Generation "Friend Me"

By Mark G. Pollock

With Antonietta Pollock

authorHOUSE®

AuthorHouse™
1663 Liberty Drive
Bloomington, IN 47403
www.authorhouse.com
Phone: 1-800-839-8640

First published by AuthorHouse 2/25/2011

ISBN: 978-1-4567-1826-8 (e)
ISBN: 978-1-4567-1827-5 (dj)
ISBN: 978-1-4567-1828-2 (sc)

Library of Congress Control Number: 2010918972

Printed in the United States of America

DEDICATION

This book is dedicated to our three children:
Adam, Christopher, and David…we love you !

Acknowledgments

We would like to pay a special acknowledgment to all of the parents out there that have devoted their lives to giving birth, raising, and loving their beautiful children!!!

CONTENTS

Introduction xi

1 The Most Precious Gift in Life...1

2 Growing Up in America as a Baby Boomer 5

3 A Parents Biggest Nightmare 15

4 "The Big 3" 19

       Cyber Bullying...21

       Sexting... 25

       Sex Predators.. 29

5 Is "Sexting" Child Pornography?...................................... 37

6 The Statistics Don't Lie 43

7 Chat Rooms 57

8 Social Media 61

9 Facebook, Love It or Hate It… It's Here to Stay!................ 67

10 What Is the Role of Our Schools? 73

11 Can You Change the Culture? 79

12 The "New" Birds and the Bees.. 87

13 Is This Big Brother? 91

14 What Do I Do Now?... 95

15 Tools for Parenting... 101

16 Cloud Parenting...A Call To All Parents! 107

17 Cloud Parenting 113

18 8 Points of Light 119

19 A Final Word to Parents 125

Acknowledgements, Disclosures, Sources, and Commentary ... 131

INTRODUCTION

There is a phenomenon going on right now in American like no other time in history. It seems as if not even a few hours goes by, let alone a day, whereby the average teen does not click a button to accept or send a "friend me" request on Facebook, or to send or receive a "tweet" on Twitter, or to quickly craft one of the 3600 text messages sent out each month on average by today's youth.

Teens are flocking in droves to be "liked" or to be "followed" and to feel as if they fit in and are part of something special. They are willing to, in essence, bare it all on the internet.

They are willing to share who they are, where they live, their personal contact information, what they like to do, where they like to go, what their hobbies are, intimate thoughts about their personalities, what music or movies they like, things going on in their lives daily or in some cases hourly, and on and on and on.

If you are reading this now and are a parent of one of these young kids, you may be one of the many in our generation that simply don't know how to handle this new generation of "digital kids." You have no reference points, may feel like you do not have many resources to turn to, and there may not be a whole lot of people with whom to share positive stories. To make matters worse, technology seems like it is moving at the speed of light and tomorrow's problems have yet to be invented, but will soon be here.

It's only been in the past several years that we have learned about "cyber bullying" and kids taking their lives in gruesome ways, or teens "sexting" nude photos of themselves and sending them to their boyfriends or girlfriends and then being charged with child pornography, or "sex predators' stalking your kids on the internet in hopes to "LMIRL" (lets meet in real life).

THE STATUS QUO IS SIMPLY NOT GOOD ENOUGH ANY MORE!

Our kids are the most precious gifts we have ever been given, and we should not let technology or the addiction to the new "social media" hype take them from us and rule their lives. Parents need constructive tools to equip themselves to adequately protect their children. It's not, as popular belief may suggest, up to our schools, or our churches or synagogues, or our counselors, movie stars, TV stars, or law enforcement or even our friends to be in charge to help our kids…its up to us…**We the Parents.**

This is the plain and simple truth.

I hope this book in some small way provides you with a few ideas or help motivate you, The Parent, into some form of action. Today's family unit needs to be of utmost importance in today's culture and the starting place to make a culture change.

Take care, good reading, and hold on to your seat!

Mark & Antonietta

1

THE MOST PRECIOUS GIFT IN LIFE

Over my adult lifetime, I have traveled over one million miles on airplanes, have been to all but four states in the USA and have spent time in over 20 countries. I have met and spent time with billionaires, CEO's of public companies, presidents of universities, teachers, pro athletes, politicians, closely held business owners, government officials, hourly plant workers, unemployed workers, the homeless, non profits, entrepreneurs, and of course other moms and dads.

I wouldn't say that I have seen it all, but I have certainly seen a lot… from the poverty of the outskirts of Egypt to the amazing riches of all that the America has to offer. I have seen the best life has to offer and also the worst. I have owned and flown on private planes and golfed some of the best courses in the world. I have hoped my checks would clear some weeks to just pay my bills and make ends meet. I have seen cancer take loved ones far too early and I have seen friends celebrate their 100th birthday.

But, with complete and total certainly, there is one experience in life that far surpasses all others and that fabulous joy is watching the birth of your child. Antonietta and I have raised three fantastic boys, all of whom were born in the same suburban hospital in an eastern suburb of Cleveland, Ohio. I was blessed to be there front and center for all three deliveries. Each one had it own sense of drama and excitement, but at the end of the day, watching our young baby slowly come out of the womb, with all of the anticipation and emotions, and then breathe his first breath…WOW, that is one experience that will forever top the rest and I one that I will never forget.

There isn't even a close second. No vacation, no trip, no enchanted land, no luxury house, no fancy watch, no boyfriend or girlfriend, no fat bank account, or any other material possession or life experience, will ever come close to that of watching the miracle of a child being born.

God absolutely knew what he was doing!

Today, throughout the world 380,000 are born each day and while 10,000 are born in America alone. There are approximately 25 millions teens between the ages of 13 and 19 and there are 15 millions "tweens," that is kids between the ages of 9 and 12. All in all, that means in America there are 40 million young children between the ages of 9 and 19.

As a parent, there was no greater priority than to do whatever you had to do to care for your child as you watched them grow from that young infant through the adolescent years and then on to adulthood. You sacrificed personal time, sleep, financial resources, emotional energy and so much more to make sure that your children had a roof over their heads, were nurtured and cared for, had clothes and food, and were properly educated.

You read books to them at night, changed their diapers, cleaned up their messes, and even talked to them about the birds and the bees. You braved the terrible two's, took them to soccer tournaments two states away while sleeping in the car, and held your breath as they learned how to drive the family car. You drove them to their first homecoming or prom date, went to hundreds of sporting events, and then sacrificed to save enough money to pay for escalating college costs.

And then, before you knew it, in what seemed like a blink of an eye, they were gone and you were empty nesters. Well, not all of you are at that stage in your lives that Antonietta and I are, but if you have any kids of your own, I know that you can relate to one or more of these pictures in your own minds eye.

Simply put, there is no greater gift and no greater responsibility that God has bestowed upon us as parents than to care for and raise up our young sons and daughters. From the moment you learn that you're pregnant, then on through birth, young childhood and through the adolescent years, there is no greater sense of joy and satisfaction than having children of your own.

2

GROWING UP IN AMERICA AS A BABY BOOMER

(And Italy too!)

Today I am squarely in the middle of the baby boomer era. I grew up in the very comfortable suburban neighborhood of Shaker Heights, Ohio. Located not too far from downtown Cleveland, our lives growing up as young kids were a blast. We walked to school every day, played kick-the-can and capture the flag with the neighborhood friends in the afternoons, and went on "bike hikes" with our shiny new 10-speeds on Saturdays.

During the summers we played little league baseball from sun up to sun down. Shaker had a great baseball league program for young kids with dozens of teams, which made for healthy competition and enabled pretty much every boy with any level of skill to fit in and play.

In fact, when I was just ten, one of the great recently retired ballplayers from the Cleveland Indians, Al Rosen, was my little league coach. Along with my dad and Ed Brandon, who later on became the CEO of National City Bank, I can remember experiencing one fun moment after another.

For example, after each game, win or lose, we would pile everyone into our brand new Ford Mustang convertible and head to the one and only McDonalds in Cleveland for a feast. Times were amazing back then. Hamburgers and fries were about 18 cents apiece and a coke was a dime. We would pull up to the outdoor window under the golden arches and order the same thing each time….two hamburgers, two fries, and a coke. And believe it or not, we would get 18 cents back from our dollar as that entire order only cost us 82 cents. Amazing isn't it when compared to today?

In those times, there were no cell phones, no computers, no game boys, no X-Box 360's, no internet, and, from my perspective, … no fears. I never once worried about meeting a sex predator on the street, being kidnapped, or losing one of my friends to suicide. From a kid's perspective we had life by the tail.

Pretty much every family in my neighborhood consisted of both a mom and dad and typically anywhere from two to five kids, usually only a few years apart. We participated in Cub Scouts and Brownies, built teepees and canoes for projects, went camping in the Smokey Mountains with our pop-up tents and campers, popped popcorn and made toasted cheese sandwiches together and watched one of only three channels on the family Black and White TV with the rabbit ears as an antenna in the one and only "family room."

While these experiences may have been unique to my family and me, I am sure that each of you could write a chapter of your unique experience and memories of your family and your youth. Maybe you played family card games, took long rides as a family, read books together or learned how to play musical instruments or even perhaps learned as a family how to cook. Whatever your story was, the common thread for me was that most everything was done as a family unit, together, whether we liked it or not.

We ate dinners together, drove to events together in the family car, and when one of us had a game, we all had a game. There were not many times for individualism and heading off into our own little worlds and doing our own things.

And a word about technology. The family technology consisted of one "family phone" located in the middle of the house. If anyone called, everyone in the house knew who it was and was able to listen to the entire conversation. There were, for most practical purposes, no private conversations. That also meant that there was no inappropriate behaviors going on or our parents were "all over us."

Family life was great for me growing up as a young child here in America. The neighborhood was fun, I had lots of friends, and we were always out playing or exploring and the only requirement was to be home for dinner at 6 p.m. Contrast that with today's youth.

As I became and adult and fell in love, it was with a beautiful young lady from Italy. Here's a little of her story because it highlights that while we are addressing life in America, these truths are universal.

Antonietta's story: (in her words)

Unlike my husband's, my childhood was quite different. I was born in Montecalvo, a small hill-town in Campania. Most of 1500 people there owned homes and land that were passed down from generation to generation. Life was very simple, unlike the sprawling cities and the millions of people that lived in nearby Naples or Rome. In fact, most people were farmers in one way or another and it was completely normal to have olive or different types of fruit trees, grape vines, and a vegetable garden just a few steps from your kitchen door.

Around the corner in our shed there were rabbits... yes, same as the French, we ate rabbits too. Chickens would also be raised mostly for personal family consumption or to be occasionally sold at the local market. My mom would go to the market on Wednesdays and come back sometimes with only four or five items that she needed for the week, such as sugar, salt, or soap.

Every now and then, my mom would bring home from the market a big fluffy sack. My curiosity led me to open the sack and see what was inside the bag as it was quite stinky and smelled a little funny, as if I had just been walking behind a herd of sheep. My mom told me not to worry, that when this freshly sheered wool had been washed, dried and pulled apart, I would like it and would soon be sleeping on a soft, comfy mattress...and she was right. I can remember today sitting in front of the fireplace and seeing how clean the wool got that we had just pulled, and that it didn't smell anymore. Each big handful looked like a cloud.

Dinnertime was very important to our family as mom always took great care to prepare a meal for us at the kitchen table. We were served a dinner of homemade bread from the wheat in her fields or tomatoes and green beans that she had just picked from the garden to make "ciambotta." A glass of homemade red wine was occasionally included in our evening meal and my mom would let us have a sip or two.

As a young girl, I loved being home and with my mom. She was always doing something around the house as her days were filled with activities such as planting a grape vineyard, hiring local workers to plant 500 olive trees in a field she purchased, making 30 or 40 bottles of tomato sauce for winter, or working on the addition to our house. Every fall, I remember pressing those grapes into wine, taking the olives to the mill to be pressed into oil, and harvesting our wheat to be turned in into flour to make bread.

Days back then seemed to last into weeks and one month seemed to me as if it was an entire year.

Our first home was very simple as it only had a kitchen and one bedroom. My sister and I slept with my mom in the same bed while my brother had a day bed with a fluffy mattress. We did not have a phone. And no, there was no computer, internet, or iPad either. No technology toys at all.

From my house on one side of the hill, I could see my school and the children playing there. School was about a 20-minute walk each day for my sister Maria, brother Felice, and me. Class went from 9:00 a.m. in the morning to 1:00pm in the afternoon. There was a special lunch program right after class ended that mom signed us up for. The lunch service was great for families whose parents worked in the fields and could not be home in time to have a warm meal prepared for their children.

Apart from all this, what I remember the most was the importance my parents placed on creating a sense of belonging and worthiness, as there was a great emphasis placed on the children being first. They took care to provide the basic necessities for us such as having food, shelter, a few pieces of clothing, and wood to heat the fire in winter to keep warm at night. Despite our lack of not having much, I did not ever feel deprived or lacking for anything at all.

Years later, after Mark and I got married, we took our first trip to Italy and I showed him the house where I lived. He was quite surprised, especially at seeing that we still had the same wool mattresses that I had helped my mom pull.

What also made my childhood a little unique is that in order to provide for our family, my Dad lived and worked in United States for eleven months of the year and for one month in the summer, he would come home and be with us. While he was gone we would talk about him with anticipation, which often started five or six months in advance of his next visit, much like the excitement today of young kids waiting for Christmas.

But for me, Dad coming back was my gift and it was so good to see him. He had, what became to me, as the "Smell of America." I think it was his American aftershave or maybe it was his Irish Spring soap or even his Hershey's chocolate he had in his suitcase for gifts to be given out to neighbors.

Like Mark I don't remember the fear of being kidnapped, molested, or bullied. In a small town such a Montecalvo, we knew pretty much everyone. When we went to weddings practically the entire town was invited for the celebration, including all of the children. And the town people looked after each other and each other's children too. If for some reason they saw some odd behavior, sooner or later, your parents knew about it.

Coming to America as a 12-year-old was exiting, yet I remember the fear of the unknown. I came in November of 1972 and the school year had already begun. My Dad quickly enrolled me into 6th grade. The superintendent, who was a friendly African American lady was kind and did her very best to help me assimilate into school.

Sensing insecurities, for the next 3 months she assigned a "buddy," Julie, to show me around school. After awhile, Julie grew a bit tired and irritated of having to be with me so much of the day and she began to distance herself. As she shared her frustration with others, I could hear the gossip starting too. I sensed that she no longer wanted this responsibility and simply wanted to do her own thing with new friends. Of course this whole experience hurt me a bit.

With support of my family though, this never become a big issue for me!

I can see now the culture in the middle and high schools today are quite different. Kids are more open in their gossip or hatred efforts, which we have now come to call "bullying." The internet has made this easier and kids can now attack each other without even being there. I wonder if being able to talk badly about someone on the Internet has made kids bolder in their attacks because it can be done with no immediate consequences or can be done with an increased amount of spite?

Having parented three boys through high school and college, I can see now how "being a little different" can create many opportunities for this behavior, just because you're not the same as them. Our boys just missed the major internet generation boom as teens, but I know that as a mom, there is no greater mission in life than to do everything in my power to protect my children and help them through these impressionable years called adolescence.

(Back to Mark)

So, as you can see, whether it was me growing up in America, or Antonietta growing up in Italy, our lives were much more simple and family oriented than the complex and fast paced internet and digital days of today.

Also, to complicate things in this generation, the "nuclear family" of the past, exists in a much different way. Since a large number of the marriages in the Untied States end up in divorce, quite a few children are living between two different families with more than one set of parents. There are step-moms and step-dads, half bothers and sisters, and blended families with many children living under one roof… as mothers and fathers re-marry. Because of these new family units, communication is both more difficult but at the same time needs to be more important between parents and children, since the needs are greater and the times together are less frequent.

Life is so different today as a parent than it was for us growing up as a baby boomer. The American family today is far from the "typical" days of the past. There is certainly an increased need to get your hands around this new thing called "the digital explosion" and then get your hands around the many dangers that come with it.

3

A PARENTS BIGGEST NIGHTMARE

Raising kids is by no means easy. Kids don't come with a "how to" manual. Much of what you learn is gained from life experiences. If you are blessed to have a mom or dad or other siblings with kids of their own nearby, they can offer invaluable advice from their own trials and tribulations.

One aspect of being a mom or dad is experiencing the intense sense of love you have for your child. My wife used to tell our boys that she would give up or do anything for them, and she did! But raising children is not all fun and games. With this commitment, comes a lot of trying experiences and moments.

There is no worse feeling than the fear of having your child kidnapped or even worse, lost to sickness or from a violent crime.

When I was a child, life was much more simple. In the last chapter, I compared and contrasted what growing up in America was like when I was young versus today. But as a parent, there is no worse negative adrenaline rush, than being out in public, your attention is diverted for just a moment, and when you turn around, your son or daughter is gone.

I can still remember being at Cedar Point with our family when the boys were young. This is the largest roller coaster amusement park in the country with the fastest and tallest rides. Well, one Saturday we were all enjoying the park and before we knew it, we turned around and Adam was gone. As our hearts pounded we rushed around frantically in a 100 yard radius until at last, we found him not too far away looking at one of the rides.

So many thoughts went through our minds, for example, what if he was kidnapped? How could we have left him out of our sights even if for only a minute? How would we ever forgive ourselves and just then, we found him.

Today, the dangers are ten fold and in an area that didn't even exist when we were parents of young kids. There are sex predators "mining" the internet sending out hundreds of thousands of messages to our teens trying to entrap them into a conversation, only to lure them to a point where they type the following message on their computer or cell phone…"LMIRL" (lets meet in real life).

There are over 1 million registered sex offenders and that only represents those that have been found and convicted of a crime.

How many more '"predators" are there going after our young tweens and teens in real life? If losing a child for a few moments at an amusement park creates an all out panic, imagine what it would feel like to have a 42-year-old man lure your 12-year-old daughter into a relationship over the internet and then meeting in person.

Or imagine what it would be like to have your 13-year-old son be bullied at school and then on Facebook or some other social media to a point where he feels that life in not worth living and to cope he decides to hang himself in the closet.

Or imagine for a moment, that your 15-year-old daughter takes a full frontal nude photo of herself and then sends it "discretely" to her boyfriend only to have it go viral on the internet the following week and everyone in school has now seen it. Maybe your son was the one that received that photo and as he forwarded it to his buddies, didn't realize that he may be prosecuted for child pornography.

Well parents…WAKE UP…THIS IS HAPPENING EVERY DAY, EVERYWHERE IN THE COUNTRY AND WITH INCREASING REGULARITY.

It is time for us as parents to take control of our kid's digital worlds and do whatever we can to prevent these tragedies from happening. It's not only the responsibility of our schools or churches or synagogues or counselors or coaches, or teachers, or best friends ….IT IS OUR RESPONSIBILITY…. WE THE PARENTS!!!

4

"THE BIG 3"

Cyber Bullying, Sexting, and Sexual Predators.
(AND A WORD ABOUT KIDNAPPING)

Cyber Bullying

According to Wikipedia, the term cyber bullying "involves the use of information and communication technologies to support deliberate, repeated, and hostile behavior by an individual or group, that is intended to harm others."

Bullying, of course, is not something new to all of us. We all remember that one "fat kid" or "gangly girl with the big glasses" that was made fun of and harassed on the school playground at recess. And, yes it hurt just as much back then and it does today.

But fast forward to present day. With the invention of the Internet, computers, and smart cell phones, bullying has been raised to a whole new form of torment. Back in the day, kids being picked on were generally limited to verbal abuse and only during the school day. Only those bully kids bold enough to look you in the eye that had the courage to harass you in person did the lions' share of the damage. Sometimes the bullying was done from a gang.

Today, it is a whole different ball game. First, bullying is not limited to the school day, its now a matter of 24 hours a day by 7 days a week by 365 days a year….in other words it never stops. Not only can the bully access you during the school day or on the bus, but now they can take the fight home and attack you on the internet or on the new age social media opportunities like Facebook, Twitter, or MySpace. There is no rest or peace of mind to the recipient of the harsh words and harassment or embarrassment caused by the bully. The innocent lives of young teens that are targets are in a constant state of attack and pain. There is nowhere to turn, no place to find solace and in many cases, what seems like to you, no options.

Also, the boldness that has emerged is staggering. Bullying is no longer done by that one or two cool kids or punks at school, it is now being done by virtually anyone. Some bullying may be innocent comments posted on Facebook by a group of friends while others may be an overt attempt to go after someone with the intent to inflict pain and hurt. Whatever the intent, the point is that it is so much easier to go on-line and post some hurtful words, like "Susie is such a slut and will sleep with anyone" or "Billy is so gay I am glad he has finally come out of the closet." You can hurt someone without having to be right there and can do it in the privacy of your bedroom on your computer and in many cases with no consequences.

The October 18, 2010 issue of *People Magazine* had as its cover headline, "Teens Suicide Tragedies. Deadly Bullying." The inside story is titled, "Tormented to Death?" The main article tells the story of Tyler Clementi, who at only 18 and just embarking on his new college career, jumped off the George Washington Bridge into the Hudson River taking his own life after learning that three days earlier his Rutgers College roommate secretly streamed a live video webcam of him having a sexual encounter with another male friend. The authorities have charged his roommate and another student with invasion of privacy which carriers a jail sentence term of five years.

According to the article, a Harris poll found that 90% of gay and lesbian teens say that they have been bullied in the past year and according to another survey, almost two thirds of the gay and lesbian community feels unsafe at school. The article goes on to mention two other 13-year-olds, Seth Walsh and Asher Brown, and 15-year-old Billy Lucas that also committed suicide in September 2010 due to being taunted for being allegedly gay or just simply different from the "rest of us." Two of the deaths were from hangings and the other shot himself. In fact, Asher was said to have been harassed for "being gay, lisping, and being Buddhist."

Imagine for a moment that at the tender age of 13, you are harassed or bullied to a point that the only option you feel is left is to take your own life. What must have been going through their young and innocent minds? The embarrassment and pain that resulted was just simply too much to handle, so the best option was not to talk it over with mom or dad, or even a friend. But a growing and tragic reality is that way too many teens are deciding to go into the privacy of a closet with a rope or with a gun or to go several hundred feet above a river and end it all with a jump.

When a teen in a small town takes his or her life, unfortunately, it's not just that person's life that is impacted. The whole town often gets involved. In early 2010, Phoebe Prince, a young intelligent and beautiful 15-year-old from a small town of 17,000 residents in South Hadley, Massachusetts ended the continual taunting by six of her school mates by hanging herself.

This case achieved national coverage on all of the TV stations as they chronicled this young girl's life as she moved from County Clare, Ireland to South Hadley here in the United States. Now this small town is trying to move on, as it has become a national focus and target of many places such as on Facebook as a "hate town."

This troubling and growing trend of cyber bullying followed by suicides just plain and simple...has to stop. But how? That's the key question, isn't it? Is this an issue to be dealt with by the kids themselves, the fellow students, the parents, the schools systems, the law enforcement community, the towns, or as it is apparent now...ALL OF THEM?!

Sexting

According to Wikipedia "sexting" is the act of sending sexually explicit messages or photographs, primarily between mobile phones. The term was first popularized around 2005, and represents the combining of sex and texting, where the latter is meant in the wide sense of sending a text possibly with images.

Sexting that involves teenagers sending explicit photographs of themselves to their peers has led to a legal gray area in countries that have strict anti-child pornography laws, such as the United States. Some teenagers who have texted photographs of themselves, or of their friends or partners, have been charged with distribution of child pornography, while those who have received the images have been charged with possession of child pornography.

In some cases the possession charge has been applied to school administrators who have investigated sexting incidents as well. The images involved in sexting are usually different in both nature and motivation from the type of content that anti-child pornography laws were created to address.

According to the latest poll, one in four teens has either sent or received a nude photo of himself or herself over a cell phone or the computer. And, that's only those that will admit to it, so my suspicions are the numbers are even worse.

This new phenomenon of taking a nude photo of yourself and sending it over the internet, for the whole world to possibly see, is simply amazing behavior. Has our culture deteriorated to such a level whereby young teens feel that in order to impress someone of the opposite sex they need to take a nude photo and send it over a medium that **WILL** be viewed at some point by hundreds, if not thousands of others? Yes, our teens are learning that while the photo may have been sent in private, sooner or later that photo will be shared with someone else and possibly even the whole Internet community.

Why are young girls, for example, committing themselves to this sort of behavior? Are they flirting with their boyfriends (or boyfriend hopefuls), are they feeling pressured, is it fun and interesting or are there some other reasons that they are partaking in this risky and potentially illegal behavior? What is going through their minds as they take out their cell phone cameras, take off their clothes, pose nude for a picture, and then send a text or email to someone who may or may not keep it private?

I was talking to an acquaintance recently that was a Boy Scout leader in a small affluent community outside of Columbus, Ohio who had a troop of a dozen boys all around 12-15 years old. During a recent camping trip, he noticed all of the boys huddled around one another as if they were calling a play in a football huddle. Not to be left out my friend squeezed his way into the "huddle" only to be shocked to see all of the commotion was around one of the boys showing off to the others, full frontal nude photos of his "new girlfriend."

Fast forward several months...the local law enforcement officers got wind of the photos and because they were sent and received by kids under age, they were considered child pornography and the boy that had the photos was now being prosecuted. What seemed like a relatively innocent series of actions has turned into a nightmare.

Back when I was young, the closet thing to this risky behavior was strip poker or spin the bottle late at night on a rare sleep over, and these episodes were far and far between. Now teens send 3,600 text messages on average each and every month, up from 3,300 last year.

That's simply amazing. Think about it. If there are 34,200 minutes in a month (after subtracting eight hours a day for sleep) that means that our teens are texting one time every 9.5 minutes while they are awake.

Have you ever been in a room full of six or seven teenage boys or girls for an evening of pizza and a movie? Take a look next time. At any one given moment, most of them will be texting someone and many of them will have three or four conversations going at one time.

Sex Predators

A sex offender (also sexual predator, sex abuser or sexual abuser) is a person who has committed a sex crime. What constitutes a sex crime differs by culture and by legal jurisdiction, but criminal offenses usually include rape, statutory rape, child sexual abuse and possessing child pornography. The term sexual predator is often used to describe severe or repeat sex offenders.

In the United States, the United Kingdom, and other countries, a convicted sex offender is often required to register with the respective jurisdiction's sex offender registry. In the U.S. registry databases are often open to the public. Sexual offenders are sometimes classified into levels. The highest-level offenders generally must register as a sex offender for their entire lives, whereas low-level offenders may only need to register for a limited time.

The term sexual predator is used to describe a person seen as obtaining or trying to obtain sexual contact with another person in a metaphorically "predatory" manner. Analogous to how a predator hunts down its prey, so the sexual predator is thought to "hunt" down his or her sex partners. People who commit sex crimes, such as rape or child sexual abuse, are commonly referred to as sexual predators, particularly in tabloid media or as a power phrase by politicians.

"Megan's Law" is an informal name for laws in the United States requiring law enforcement authorities to make information available to the public regarding registered sex offenders. Individual states decide what information will be made available and how it should be disseminated. Commonly included information includes the offender's name, picture, address, incarceration date, and nature of crime. The information is often displayed on free public websites, but can be published in newspapers, distributed in pamphlets, or through various other means.

At the Federal level, Megan's Law is known as the Sexual Offender (Jacob Wetterling) Act of 1994, and requires people convicted of sex crimes against children to notify local law enforcement of any change of address or employment after release from custody, prison, or a psychiatric facility. The notification requirement may be imposed for a fixed period of time usually at least ten years or permanently.

Some states may legislate registration for all sex crimes, even if no minors were involved. It is a felony in most jurisdictions to fail to register or fail to update information.

Megan's Law provides two major information services to the public: sex offender registration and community notification. The details of what is provided as part of sex offender registration and how community notification is handled vary from state to state, and in some states the required registration information and community notification protocols have changed many times since Megan's Law was passed. The Adam Walsh Child Protection and Safety Act supplements Megan's Law with new registration requirements and a three-tier system for classifying sex offenders according to their risk to the community.

Kidnapping

According to Wikipedia, in criminal law, kidnapping is the taking away or transportation of a person against the person's will, usually to hold the person in false imprisonment, a confinement without legal authority. This may be done for ransom or in furtherance of another crime, or in connection with a child custody dispute.

According to the FBI, there are 837,055 missing persons in the U.S. and estimates are that 80 percent are children. Somewhere around 99 percent of these kids were found within hours or days by usual law enforcement response. The rest go missing for prolonged periods of time.

No greater public display of this horrendous crime was the case of Jaycee Lee Dugard who was kidnapped on June 10, 1991 at the tender age of just 11 years old. Jaycee was abducted from a school bus stop within plain view of her home in South Lake Tahoe, California. She went missing for over 18 years until found on August 26, 2009. Her captors repeatedly raped her over this period and during her time in captivity and she had 2 children.

Another kidnapping that was displayed all over the news was the case of the Elizabeth Smart kidnapping, which occurred on June 5, 2002. At the age of 14, she was abducted from her Salt Lake City, Utah bedroom.

On March 12, 2003, just over nine months after the abduction, Brian David Mitchell who was wanted by police for questioning, was spotted traveling with two companions, just a mere 18 miles from Elizabeth's home. An alert biker, who had heard of the kidnapping on America's Most Wanted the night before, notified police.

As it turned out, one of the companions was Elizabeth Smart who was disguised in a gray wig, sunglasses, and veil. Her abduction and recovery were widely reported and was the subject of a made-for-television movie and a published book.

It doesn't get much worse than these two heinous crimes of abduction and kidnapping. While kidnapping may not be as rampant as the "Big 3" mentioned earlier in the chapter, it is important for parents to be prepared for in advance for a potential kidnapping.

For example, one of the products in the tools chapter has a GPS locator as part of its basic service, and many cell phone carriers also sell this feature. While a remote possibility, why not purchase a phone with this service available and have it live in case the worst does happen?

Additionally, know what to do in the event your child goes missing or you believe he was kidnapped. The first hour is the most critical time after an abduction occurs. Be prepared to notify authorities, have photos and identifiable items ready, and to the best of your ability remain calm and help the law enforcement do their jobs.

We have now learned a little bit more about the "BIG 3" fears out there: sexting, cyber bullying, and sex predators as well as kidnapping too. What we do with this information is up to us. We are now perhaps a little more educated and a little more exposed to the issues at hand for our kids and our families. But, at the end of the day, we now need to develop an action plan custom tailored to our individual family and then put it into action.

5

IS "SEXTING" CHILD PORNOGRAPHY?

As we have seen from all of the statistics, teenagers are sending and receiving sexual messages and naked pictures of themselves to their boyfriends and girlfriends in record numbers. In more cases than not, it's the girl sending a picture or message to a guy friend, but not certainly limited to just girls.

Perhaps the most amazing thought of all is that, while most parents feel this behavior is totally inappropriate and are somewhat astonished at the practice, the teens engaged in "sexting" don't really see anything wrong with it.

Their common response has been "What's the big deal?"

Well, from a reputation perspective it is a big deal. From a legal perspective it could be even a bigger deal! In fact, this practice of "sexting" can in some cases ruin our teenagers' lives, particularly if law enforcement gets involved.

If you asked the average parent if sending a nude photo by their teen is illegal, they are likely to say, "I don't know." If you asked the average teen if it is illegal, the likely answer is, "of course not, why are you even asking me?"

When you look around the country there are teens being prosecuted in many states in record numbers. If you are unsure about what I am talking about, just look at the evening news, read a national newspaper or do a Google search on this topic on your internet browser and watch what comes up.

For example, a young 13-year-old teenage boy in Ohio is being prosecuted for a felony after being caught taping a sex act between he and a male friend and then unveiling it to some friends at a skating party. He is now being charged, in essence, with a child pornography charge. If convicted, he will be labeled a sex offender, something that will impact his life in an incredibly negative way... forever.

So as these cases are becoming more and more prevalent, we are seeing kids kicked out of school, off of sports teams, and prosecuted for crimes. When exposed to the public, these young lives are changed in a way that will influence their paths forever.

The state and local legislators have to respond and react to this growing problem. There seem to be two general theories emerging; one thought is the "leave no prisoners" theory. That is, law enforcement, attorneys, and our judges believe that in order to stop this practice in its roots, there needs to be a tough stance and there cannot be any gray lines. "You committed a crime and you need to pay the penalty." A naked picture of an underage child sent over the internet, is at its core, considered child pornography and needs to be treated as such.

For example, in Orlando Florida, an young girl sexted a nude photo of herself to then boyfriend Phillip Alpert, who in turn, after they broke up, distributed it in a mass email to hundreds of people as a way to get back at her. He was convicted of transmission of child pornography and is now a sex offender and is required to hold that label until he turns 43. Since his dad lives near a school, he cannot even move in his house. Do you think that single act changed his life forever?

In another case, there are a number of 14 and 15-year-old females at Greensburg Salem High School in Greensburg, PA that are all facing charges of manufacturing, disseminating or possessing child pornography. The boys, who received the photos and who are 16 and 17, face charges of possession, according to an article published by WPXI-TV in Pittsburgh.

Police indicated that the photos were discovered after school officials seized a cell phone from one of the students who was using it in violation of school rules and found a nude photo of a classmate on it. As police were called in and they did their investigation, other phones containing nude photos were discovered too.

In the WPXI story, law enforcement is noted as stating that they "decided to file the child pornography charges to send a strong message to other minors who might consider sending such photos to friends."

The other thought process emerging is one that is far more lenient. In essence, the thought process is that these are just young kids that don't really understand what they are doing and the laws are far too harsh. Instead of felonies these acts should be punishable with misdemeanors or with community service and lots of education. But, certainly not by ruining the kids lives forever and lumping them into the harsh worlds of adult sex offenders and common criminals. To prosecute these kids is "overkill" and the laws need to be changed to reflect this new soft criminal activity.

According to one study, and there are many, 39% of teens between ages of 13 to 19 are sending, posting, or receiving sexually suggestive messages of themselves on an IM, email, or text message and 20% are nude or semi-nude photos of themselves.

And why are our kids sexting, posting nude photos on emails in the first place. Again, most studies say they are doing this innocently either in hopes to get or keep a boyfriend/girlfriend or they are being pressured into doing it.

Whatever the reasons though, these practices simply need to be stopped. What the kids don't realize it that childhood relationships last such a short time and when breakups occur, the person in possession of risqué information WILL NOT likely keep it private. Once out there in the cloud (on the internet), it is simply out there forever.

6

THE STATISTICS DON'T LIE

Cyber Bullying

According to an i-Safe America survey of 4th-8th graders (yes, please note this is not even high school kids) a few years back, here are some statistics on Cyber Bullying. There are many such surveys done in recent years.

+ 42% of kids have been bullied while online. one in four have had it happen more than once.
+ 35% of kids have been threatened online. Nearly one in five have had it happen more than once.
+ 21% of kids have received mean or threatening e-mail or other messages.
+ 58% of kids admit someone has said mean or hurtful things to them online. More than four out of ten say it has happened more than once.

+ 53% of kids admit having said something mean or hurtful to another person online. More than one in three have done it more than once.
+ 58% have not told their parents or an adult about something mean or hurtful that happened to them online.

Cyber Bullying Tips

+ Tell a trusted adult about the bullying, and keep telling them until the adult takes action.
+ Don't open or read messages by cyber bullies.
+ Tell your school if it is school related. Schools should have a bullying solution in place.
+ Don't erase the messages—they may be needed to take action.
+ Protect yourself—never agree to meet with the person or with anyone you meet online.
+ If bullied through chat or instant messaging, the "bully" can often be blocked.
+ If you are threatened with harm, inform the local police.

Sexting

Everyone is talking about sexting these days. From a study from "Sex and Tech" here are some of the results from a Survey of Teens and Young Adults done in a Q&A format.

+ **How many young adults are sending or posting nude or semi-nude images of themselves?**
  + 31% of young adult
  + 33% of young adults overall
  + 36% of young adult men

+ **How many teens say they have sent/posted nude or semi-nude pictures or video of themselves?**
  + 20% of teens overall

+ 22% of teen girls
+ 18% of teen boys
+ 11% of young teen girls (ages 13-16)

+ **Sexually suggestive messages (text, email, IM) are even more prevalent than sexually suggestive images. How many teens are sending or posting sexually suggestive messages?**

  + 39% of all teens
  + 37% of teen girls
  + 40% of teen boys
  + 48% of teens say they have received such messages

+ **How many young adults are sending or posting sexually suggestive messages?**

  + 59% of all young adults
  + 56% of young adult women
  + 62% of young adult men
  + 64% of young adults say they have received such messages
  + 71% of teen girls and 67% of teen guys who have sent or posted sexually suggestive content say they have sent/posted this content to a boyfriend/girlfriend.
  + 21% of teen girls and 39% of teen boys say they have sent such content to someone they wanted to date or hook up with.
  + 15% of teens who have sent or posted nude/semi-nude images of themselves say they have done so to someone they only knew online.
  + 21% of young adult women and 30% of young adult men

who have sent/posted sexually suggestive content have done so to someone they wanted to date or hook up with.

+ 15% of young adult women and 23% of young adult men who have sent sexually suggestive material say they have done so to someone they only knew online.

+ **How common is it to share sexy messages and images with those other than the intended recipient?**

   + 44% of both teen girls and teen boys say it is common for sexually suggestive text messages to get shared with people other than the intended recipient.

   + 36% of teen girls and 39% of teen boys say it is common for nude or semi-nude photos to get shared with people other than the intended recipient.

   + 44% of young adult women and 50% of young adult men say it is common for sexually suggestive text messages to get shared with people other than the intended recipient.

   + 48% of young adult women and 46% of young adult men say it is common for nude or semi-nude photos to get shared with people other than the intended recipient.

+ **Does sending sexually suggestive text and images affect what happens in real life?**

   + 22% of teens and 28% of young adults say they are personally more forward and aggressive using sexually suggestive words and images than they are in "real life."

   + 38% of teens and 40% of young adults say exchanging

sexually suggestive content makes dating or hooking up with others more likely.

+ 29% of teens and 24% of young adults believe those exchanging sexually suggestive content are "expected" to date or hook up.

+ **How do teens and young adults feel about sending/posting sexually suggestive content?**

  + 75% of teens and 71% of young adults say sending sexually suggestive content "can have serious negative consequences."

  + Yet, 39% of teens and 59% of young adults have sent or posted sexually suggestive emails or text messages — and 20% of teens and 33% of young adults have sent/posted nude or semi-nude images of themselves.

+ **How many teens and young adults say they have been shown nude/semi-nude content originally meant for someone else?**

  + 38% of teen girls and 39% of teen boys say they have had sexually suggestive text messages or emails—originally meant for someone else—shared with them.

  + 25% of teen girls and 33% of teen boys say they have had nude or semi-nude images—originally meant for someone else—shared with them.

  + 37% of young adult women and 47% of young adult men have had sexually suggestive text messages or emails—intended for someone else—shared with them.

+ 24% of young adult women and 40% of young adult men say they have had nude or semi-nude images—originally meant for someone else—shared with them.

+ **Why do teens and young adults send or post sexually suggestive content?**

    + 51% of teen girls say pressure from a guy is a reason girls send sexy messages or images; only 18% of teen boys cited pressure from female counterparts as a reason.

    + 23% of teen girls and 24% of teen boys say they were pressured by friends to send or post sexual content. Talk to your kids about what they are doing in cyber-space.

+ **Among teens who have sent sexually suggestive content:**

    + 66% of teen girls and 60% of teen boys say they did so to be "fun or flirtatious"— their most common reason for sending sexy content.

    + 52% of teen girls did so as a "sexy present" for their boyfriend.

    + 44% of both teen girls and teen boys say they sent sexually suggestive messages or images in response to such content they received.

    + 40% of teen girls said they sent sexually suggestive messages or images as "a joke."

    + 34% of teen girls say they sent/posted sexually suggestive content to "feel sexy."

    + 12% of teen girls felt "pressured" to send sexually suggestive messages or images and ignore the potential short-term and long-term consequences of their actions.

Statistics regarding Facebook:

People on Facebook

+ More than 500 million active users
+ 50% of our active users log on to Facebook in any given day
+ Average user has 130 friends
+ People spend over 700 billion minutes per month on Facebook

Activity on Facebook

+ There are over 900 million objects that people interact with (pages, groups, events and community pages)
+ Average user is connected to 80 community pages, groups and events
+ Average user creates 90 pieces of content each month
+ More than 30 billion pieces of content (web links, news stories, blog posts, notes, photo albums, etc.) shared each month

Global Reach

+ More than 70 translations available are available on the site

+ About 70% of Facebook users are outside the United States
+ Over 300,000 users helped translate the site through the translations application

Platform

+ More than one million developers and entrepreneurs from more than 180 countries
+ Every month, more than 70% of Facebook users engage with Platform applications
+ More than 550,000 active applications currently on Facebook Platform
+ More than one million websites have integrated with Facebook Platform
+ More than 150 million people engage with Facebook on external websites every month
+ Two-thirds of comScore's U.S. Top 100 websites and half of comScore's Global Top 100 websites have integrated with Facebook

Mobile

+ There are more than 200 million active users currently accessing Facebook through their mobile devices
+ People that use Facebook on their mobile devices are twice as active on Facebook than non-mobile users
+ There are more than 200 mobile operators in 60 countries working to deploy and promote Facebook mobile products

Sex Predators

According to the NBC news program Dateline, as of January 2006, law enforcement officials estimate that as many as 50,000 sexual predators are online at any given moment.

According to the National Institute of Mental Health, the typical sex offender molests an average of 117 children, most of whom do not report the offenses.

And, believe it or not, 95% of perpetrators know their victims.

It is estimated that about 71% of child sex offenders are under the age of 35 and know the victim at least casually; 80% fall into a normal intelligence category and 59% gain sexual access through seduction or enticement.

7

CHAT ROOMS

According to Wikipedia, the term **chat room**, or **chatroom**, is primarily used by mass media to describe any form of synchronous conferencing, occasionally even asynchronous conferencing. The term can thus mean any technology ranging from real-time online chat over instant messaging and online forums to fully immersive graphical social environments.

A chat room is a Web site, part of a Web site, or part of an online service such as America Online, which provides a venue for communities of users with a common interest to communicate in real time. Forums and discussion groups, in comparison, allow users to post messages but don't have the capacity for interactive messaging.

Most chat rooms don't require users to have any special software; those that do, such as Internet Relay Chat (IRC) allow users to download it from the Internet. Chat room users register for the chat room of their choice, choose a user name and password, and log into a particular room (most sites have multiple chat rooms).

Inside the chat room, generally there is a list of the people currently online, who also are alerted that another person has entered the chat room. To chat, users type a message into a text box. The message is almost immediately visible in the larger communal message area and other users respond. Users can enter chat rooms and read messages without sending any, a practice known as lurking.

So what's all of the beef about chat rooms? Well, if as a parent you have never gone to a chat room, humor yourself a bit and just go to any on-line chat and see what happens. Maybe just type in a sexy name for yourself as a15-year-old girl "looking for friendship."

Well, just in case you don't indulge yourself before finishing this book, here's what will happen. In less than a matter of minutes, one or more sex predators will come out of the woodwork and engage you into a conversation.

It will usually be "R-rated" and fast and furious. They will get right to the point and then try to lure you into a long term relationship "off-line" or maybe they will ask you to "go private."

Another danger of chatrooms is that many people who visit chat rooms will use them as a place to experience online "cybersex" or computer love. While you can't physically see the other partner, users derive stimulation from descriptive text.

Many Internet chat and messaging services allow users to display or send each other photos of themselves and users may chose to exchange nude or sexual photos. This has led to widespread concern about the potential for the sexual exploitation of minors. And once again, we have learned that kids under the legal age of their state who take sexually suggestive or explicit digital photos of themselves and share such photos with others may be subject to prosecution under child-pornography statutes.

One of the scariest places today on the internet is a site called Chatroulette. This is a website that pairs random strangers from around the world together for webcam-based conversations. Visitors to the website randomly begin an online video plus audio chat with another visitor. At any point, either user may leave the current chat by initiating another random connection.

The Chatroulette web site was created by Andrey Ternovskiy, a 17-year-old high school student in Moscow, Russia. Ternovskiy says the concept arose from video chats he used to have with friends on Skype, and that he wrote the first version of Chatroulette in "two days and two nights". Ternovskiy chose the name "Chatroulette" after watching The Deer Hunter, a 1978 film set in the Vietnam War in which prisoners of war are forced to play Russian roulette.

In early November 2009, shortly after the site launched, it had 500 visitors per day. One month later there were 50,000. The site has been featured in The New York Times, New York Magazine, Good Morning America, Newsnight in the United Kingdom, and on The Daily Show with Jon Stewart.

In February 2010, there were about 35,000 people on Chatroulette at any given time. Around the beginning of March, Ternovskiy estimated the site to have around 1.5 million users, approximately 33% of them from the United States and 5% from Germany.

I was talking to someone that visited this site for awhile and he indicated that one out of every 10 "random" users that enter the site was an older man often without any clothes on. Talk about a scary scene for our kids. Even if this kind of site is visited, even once, out of curiosity to see what all the hype is about, you never know where that could lead our kids.

Chat rooms are dangerous and live so parents be aware of these sites and be prepared to talk to your children about them as part of your internet dangers dialogue.

8

SOCIAL MEDIA

Social media has been tossed around left and right in today's home, the news, and in business. What exactly is "Social Media?" In the olds days before the internet, the "Media" was either the newspaper, the radio, or other print advertisements like magazines. In essence, media was an instrument of communication to the people.

However, the key difference between media back then and that which exists today, is that the media as we used to know it (newspapers, TV and radio) was only one-way. That is, there was no interaction as it was all one way. The "Media" printed and we read.

Today, social media on the internet is far different. It is not only a two-way communication but at the core of its popularity is the fact that the communications are interactive.

Social media websites don't just give you information, but they interact with you live while giving you the information needed from that particular venue. This interaction can be as simple as voting on a topic of interest that others "like" too and sharing photos to as complex as setting up whole profiles and communications live via chats such as Facebook or MySpace.

According to Wikipedia, social media are media for social interaction, using highly accessible and scalable publishing techniques. Social media uses web-based technologies to turn communication into interactive dialogues. Social media is also defined as "a group of Internet-based applications that build on the ideological and technological foundations of Web 2.0, which allows the creation and exchange of user-generated content." Businesses also refer to social media as consumer-generated media (CGM). A common thread running through all definitions of social media is a blending of technology and social interaction for the co-creation of value.

There are many reasons for the boom in social media usage for individuals around the world. Here are some interesting statistics about how popular social media has become in the country:

- Social networking now accounts for 22% of all time spent online in the U.S.
- A total of 234 million people age 13 and older in the U.S. used mobile devices in December 2009 and accessed a social site.

+ Twitter has 175 million users and processes nearly 800,000 queries a day.
+ Twitter processed more than one billion tweets in December 2009 and averages almost 65 million tweets per day in 2010.
+ Over 25% of U.S. internet page views occurred at one of the top social sites.

Social media sites on the internet come in many different flavors. Here are some of the popular types or categories of sites:

+ Internet forums
+ Weblogs
+ Social blogs
+ Microblogging
+ Wikis
+ Podcasts
+ Photographs or picture sharing
+ Video
+ Rating and social bookmarking
+ Gaming or games
+ Virtual communities
+ Crowdsourcing
+ Music sharing

Today, a social media user will decide in four seconds whether or not he or she will interact with you. This is particularly important when using social media for business. Imagine having only four seconds to make your pitch for your product before losing the customer or before they become disengaged!

What ever happen to the 60 second "elevator pitch?"

Blogs

Let's look at one of the up and coming types of social media other than Facebook or Twitter, which dominates most of the categories of popularity or usage. Since we have addressed many of the other main topics in this book, let's look for a moment at Blogs.

According to Wikipedia, the term "blog," which is a blend of the term web log, is a type website usually maintained by an individual with regular entries of commentary, descriptions of events, or other material such as graphics or video. Entries are commonly displayed in reverse-chronological order. Blog can also be used as a verb, meaning, "to maintain or add content to a blog."

Most blogs are interactive and allow visitors to leave comments and even message each other via widgets on the blogs and it is this interactivity that distinguishes them from other static websites.

People use blogs as personal diaries, to have current information about a topic of interest, to interact with other experts, view and share photos, videos, or music and a whole lot of other common sites on a particular subject. A typical blog combines text, images, and links to other blogs.

One of the issues rising up from Blogs in general occurs with teens and college students in particular. With so many interactive online diaries or personal blogs, the daily lives of these young kids are playing out in front of their very eyes, and minute by minute in lots of cases.

Today, people are meeting on line and then breaking up on line. People are making friends on line and then fighting with those same individuals on line. Unfortunately, with the ease of use and barriers to entry, young kids are also meeting strangers on line. It is incredibly easy for a 10 or 15-year-old to boot up their computer, enter into a chatroom or someone's blog area and then simply "meet" someone. You don't know who that person is, what their age is, if they are a criminal or not...nothing, other than what they tell you. And, how do you discern fact from fiction?

We could go on and on about social media, but I think you all get the point. There are increasingly popular trends on the internet today and certainly Blogs are one of them. Our goal here was to simply introduce the topic to help expand your awareness of these types of sites and then by being more informed you will have a better grasp on how to handle this new media in the future.

9

FACEBOOK, LOVE IT OR HATE IT...
IT'S HERE TO STAY!

According to Wikipedia, Facebook is a social network service and website launched in February 2004 that is operated and privately owned by Facebook, Inc. As of July 2010 Facebook has more than 500 million active users, which is about one person for every fourteen in the world. Users may create a personal profile, add other users as friends and exchange messages, including automatic notifications when they update their profile.

Additionally, users may join common interest user groups, organized by workplace, school, college, or other characteristics. The name of the service stems from the colloquial name for the book given to students at the start of the academic year by university administrations in the U.S. with the intention of helping students to get to know each other better. Facebook allows anyone who declares themselves to be at least 13 years old to become a registered user of the website.

Facebook was founded by Mark Zuckerberg with his college roommates and fellow computer science students Eduardo Saverin, Dustin Moskovitz and Chris Hughes. The website's membership was initially limited by the founders to Harvard students, but was expanded to other colleges in the Boston area, the Ivy League, and Stanford University. It gradually added support for students at various other universities before opening to high school students, and, finally, to anyone aged 13 and over.

Facebook has met with some controversy. It has been blocked intermittently in several countries including Pakistan, Syria, the People's Republic of China, Vietnam, Iran, Uzbekistan, and North Korea. It has also been banned at many places of work to discourage employees from wasting time using the service. Facebook's privacy has also been an issue and the safety of their users has been compromised several times. Facebook settled a lawsuit regarding claims over source code and intellectual property.

A January 2009 Compete.com study ranked Facebook as the most used social network by worldwide monthly active users, followed by MySpace. Entertainment Weekly put it on its end-of-the-decade "best-of" list, saying, "How on earth did we stalk our exes, remember our co-workers' birthdays, bug our friends, and play a rousing game of Scrabble before Facebook?" Quantcast estimates Facebook has 135.1 million monthly unique U.S. visitors

As you can see above, nearly one in every 14 people in the world has a Facebook page. One of the most quoted reasons that parents are afraid of the internet for their kids is the whole social medium issue which includes Facebook, MySpace, YouTube, and the like.

Why is it so scary for parents? Is fear of the unknown driving this concern or some other reasons?

So lets dig into Facebook a little bit more and see how to best approach this site as a parent concerned about his or her child using it. Lets call this part:

Facebook 101

What are the main components of Facebook?

1. **Personal Profile**: everyone starts out loading in certain information about themselves. This includes their personal information, photos, groups, schedule and their wall.

2. **Friends**: These are all of the people that you have contacted (or vice versa) that have agreed to be your friend and thus you both have the ability to view each others site.

3. **Events**: Users can create and post events and invite other's to them.

4. **Personal invitations**: Individuals can be sent invitations to the various events or they can be listed as open to everyone. There is also an RSVP feature that can be part of your event posting.

5. **Messages**: This is where any user can send an internal email

message from any Facebook member to another Facebook member.

6. **Poke**: This feature allows a user to send a message via Facebook to another user stating that they have been "poked" or in essence "notified" by the other that they have reached out to them.

7. **Wall**: The 'wall" is the part on each users page that represents a place or message board whereby any other user can post a public message for anyone to read. These messages can be edited by the user whose profile the message was posted to. The writer's picture of who sent message appears next to the post.

8. **Photos**: The user's photos appear on the profile page and are also attached to the writer's messages.

9. **My Photo Page**: The user of each account can post photos in "albums" and the user can label people in their albums and the user can also "tag" people in the pictures to tie those people to their specific page.

10. **Advertisements**: Individuals or corporations can buy space to post advertisements, which generate revenue for Facebook.

11. **Pulse Page**: Here is where the "Top 10" lists are generated from the Facebook community and other trend driven features.

What is the Good, the Bad, and the Ugly of Facebook?

First, the Good: The most unique and positive feature of Facebook is that the site is totally free, thus explaining part of the explosion in its growth. This site is a invaluable tool to locate and follow friends, find others that share similar interests or hobbies, to be used as a great educational tool, and in many cases it's simply a fun, interesting and efficient way to keep in touch with your world of friends.

Second, the Bad: Two of the most noted downfalls of Facebook has been the "whole safety" concern around the public nature of the information being available to pretty much anyone. The second concern is that users of the site waste an enormous amount of time per day using it. Some kids spend hours on their Facebook pages each day!

If you post anything to your account, it is there for everyone to see and once it gets into the pubic domain, it is there forever. You cannot take back something you post on line.

Third, the Ugly: Perhaps the biggest concern that exists, and one we are most concerned about here in this book in our quest, is that social media sites are a plethora of information for predators. In a matter of moments, a predator can find out your name, your contact information, where you live, where you go to school, what are your hobbies, who your friends are and so much more…get the picture?

What can I do as a responsible Facebook user and parent?

First, teach your kids to be smart users of the site. They need to be aware of all of the safety concerns of the public internet and how information and photos can be used. Second, Make sure that you and your kids fully understand all of the privacy features built into the site. There are different levels of privacy filtering in addition to the custom features on your individual sites.

There is a blocking feature that can keep certain individuals from being able to view your site and your individual profile. And finally there are features that can be turned on an off that will help keep certain aspects of your information private to only you.

If you haven't spent much time learning about Facebook, then take the time…it will only benefit you and your family now and in the future!

10

WHAT IS THE ROLE OF OUR SCHOOLS?

Apart from our main role as a parent, the next logical question we all ask ourselves is, "What should be the role of our schools?" when it comes to all aspects of policing or teaching about the dangers of cyber bullying, sexting, and sex predators?

I think as each year goes by, what roles schools should play get more blurred. There has always been a debate about what does it mean to "separate the church from the state" as it relates to what role should school play in relationship to teaching religion, saying the pledge of allegiance and things of this nature.

There are constant battles going on each year about the topics and subjects that should be in our textbooks. The debate rages on as to what ages should schools be teaching "sex education" to our kids.

Should our first graders be exposed to what the "body parts" are all about or what does an "alternative lifestyle" mean?

But when it comes to the dangers of the digital world, which has come on fast and furious, many schools are like deer stuck in headlights or birds with their heads in the sand. Many just simply don't know what to do about it.

Take for example, Mentor High, one of Ohio's largest school systems and located only 30 minutes from where I live. Over the past few years, Mentor High has experienced several incredible tragedies as four students have taken their own lives.

One of my friends, who is a pastor in that township, had the life-changing experience of presiding over one of these funerals. He said that the image is a heartbreaking one as he looked down and saw the open casket of a 16-year-old who no longer viewed life worth living. Sladjana Vidovic, one of the lost teens, was portrayed in an recent AP article posted online as this, "She lay there in an her casket, dressed in the sparkly pink dress she had intended to wear to prom." This tragic ending to an amazing young life occurred three more times that year at Mentor High School.

What was the common thread here? All were victims of bullying. As reported to the papers Vidovic, a native Croatian, was teased for her accent and called "Slutty Jana;" a second was harassed for having a learning disability, another for being gay, a fourth for being a boy who wore pink.

As a result of these tragedies, two families, including the Vidovics, are suing the school district. According to the allegations, Vidovic's parents reportedly begged the school to intervene many times, and say it promised to take care of Sladjana. When they asked to see records related to their reports of bullying, the school said they were destroyed during a switch in computer systems. According to Sladjana's sister, the girls who had tormented her for months walked up to the casket and laughed. Some students that were interviewed say the problem is Mentor's culture of conformity: "If you're not an athlete or cheerleader, you're not cool. And if you're not cool, you're a prime target for the bullies"

Or take the case of one of the other students, Eric Mohat, who called himself "The Insane Optimistic Musician" on MySpace and was simply referred to as "Twiggy" to family and friends.

After months of persistent bullying in math class, the 17-year-old shot himself in the head, according to a federal lawsuit filed the day before his suicide's two-year anniversary.

The lawsuit claims that a fellow classmate and within hearing distance of his math teacher, told Eric that day, "Why don't you go home and shoot yourself? No one would miss you."

Bill and Janis, Eric's parents, are having an extremely difficult time coping with the loss who filed the suit. "We're barely functioning," said his father, who still gets nightmares.

"I don't even want to get into what it's like being the parents of a suicide victim. That's a special brand of hell." Filed in the U.S. District Court for the Northern District of Ohio, the lawsuit requests a trial by jury, which could take about a year to materialize, said Kenneth D. Myers, the family's attorney.

It alleges the school district violated Eric's civil right to safety, as well as the family's 14th Amendment rights to raise and educate Eric in a safe environment. The Mentor School Board, Superintendent Jacqueline Hoynes, High School Principal Joe Spiccia and math teacher Thomas Horvath are all listed as defendants.

Myers said the Mohat family has requested whatever monetary relief possible, but not for themselves.

"They've decided that if they got any money they'd find some use for it," Myers said, "like paying for training programs or a scholarship fund in Eric's name, some sort of good works that will help get the message out."

In Eric's case, the bullying started with teasing, verbal intimidation and name-calling. Words like "gay," "queer" and "homo" were initially used but it soon lead to pushing, shoving and hitting in the classroom and hallways, again according to the lawsuit. Myers said the family's lawsuit is somewhat unprecedented.

"I haven't seen a specific case that involved a school suicide, but I know there definitely are cases that have been brought and won regarding bullying in schools and the school's obligations to keep students safe," he said.

In a press release, the schools system said the following, "Mentor Public Schools takes all claims of bullying and harassment seriously and continues to train staff and students using a robust anti-bullying program, implemented in all 14 schools. The district is also committed to raising awareness among students and staff of depressive illness and suicide prevention."

A pilot program at the high school, "Give a Hand Take a Hand," has resulted in an eight-student peer-to-peer suicide awareness team that began presenting to ninth- and 10th-graders in February, assisted by the Lake County Suicide Prevention Coalition, the release continues.

While Mentor High is certainly unique in the number of suicides in one school and in a two-year period, it does point out the complexity of these issues that are becoming a growing problem across America.

So as it related to schools and their roles, while much of the groundwork needs to start in the homes, much of the battleground or ground zero occurs at the schools. In response then, the school systems need to develop a robust strategy of how to approach and address these issues. Some schools, as Mentor claims, have programs in place now and are actively promoting them, while others are just getting started.

With our increasingly litigious society, the schools need to act swiftly and put in place all possible measures to educate, train, and execute programs to handle the ever-changing problems that their students face on a daily basis.

A zero tolerance policy needs to be implemented and clearly communicated to everyone in the community, starting with the students themselves, then to the teachers and staff, and then on to the parents and everyone else.

Next to the parents and the kid's homes, the schools play the next most important role, as this is where the children spend most of their time and where they meet up with most of their friends. Lets get active with our school systems and help them in any way possible. Don't let this burden fall on their shoulders alone.

11

CAN YOU CHANGE THE CULTURE?

I heard a phrase recently...."what one generation tolerates, the next one embraces." That couldn't be any more true for the changing culture from my generation of the baby boomers to that of gen-x and gen-y. Generation X, commonly abbreviated to Gen X, is the generation born after the baby boom ended. While there is no universally agreed upon time frame, the term generally includes people born from the late 1960's to the late 1970's and early 1980's, usually not later than 1981. The term had also been used in different times and places for various different subcultures or countercultures since the 1950s. Here is a brief summary of the various generations since 1914.

+ **The Lost Generation**, primarily known as the Generation of 1914 in Europe, is a term originating with Gertrude Stein to describe those who fought in World War I.

+ **The Greatest Generation**, also known as the G.I. Generation, is the generation that includes the veterans who fought in World War II. They were born from around 1901 to 1924, coming of age during the Great Depression. Journalist Tom Brokaw dubbed this the Greatest Generation in a book of the same name.

+ **The Silent Generation,** born 1925 to 1945 is the generation that includes those who were too young to join the service during World War II. Many had fathers who served in World War I. Generally recognized as the children of the Great Depression; this event during their formative years had a profound impact on them.

+ **The Baby Boom Generation** is the generation that was born following World War II, about 1946 up to approximately 1964, a time that was marked by an increase in birth rates. The baby boom has been described variously as a "shockwave" and as "the pig in the python" By the sheer force of its numbers, the boomers were a demographic bulge, which remodeled society as it passed through it. In general, baby boomers are associated with a rejection or redefinition of traditional values; however, many commentators have disputed the extent of that rejection, noting the widespread continuity of values with older and younger generations.

In Europe and North America boomers are widely associated with privilege, as many grew up in a time of affluence. One of the features of Boomers was that they tended to think of themselves as a special generation; very different from those that had come before them. In the 1960s, as the relatively large numbers of young people became teenagers and young adults, they, and those around them, created a very specific rhetoric around their cohort, and the change they were bringing about.

+ **Generation X** is the generation generally defined as those born after the baby boom ended, and hence sometimes referred to as Baby Busters, with earliest birth dates seen used by researchers ranging from 1961 to the latest 1981 at its greatest extent.

+ **Generation Y** is also known as **Millennial Generation**, Generation Next, or Echo Boomer. The earliest suggested birth dates ranging from mid to late 1970s to the latest in the early 2000s Today, many follow William Strauss and Neil Howe's theories in defining the Millennials. They use the start year as 1982, and end years around the turn of the millennium. Generation Z, also known as Generation I or Internet Generation, and dubbed the "Digital Natives," is the following generation. The earliest birth is generally dated in the early 1990s.

The activities and actions of teens today that would have been thought taboo in earlier generations are openly embraced and even flaunted in public, on TV and of course in Hollywood. Just look at Lindsay Lohan, Paris Hilton, Madonna, Charlie Sheen, Britney Spears, Heidi Montag, and so many others that have become role models for our young kids.

If you don't know the power these celebrities have over our kids, just take your young teen to a Jonas Brothers or Miley Cyrus concert and just look around and watch (and likely in amazement).

There is no greater example than what I am referring to than the enormously popular TV show Glee. This show, a group of 10 teen kids from William McKinley High School in California, has drawn as many as 14 million viewers in one evening and has won a Golden Globe, was recently nominated for a record-setting 19 Emmys, a Screen Actors Guild award, a Peoples Choice award, and had a record 25 singles hit the Billboard Hot 100 charts in 2009. That is the most single hits since the Beatles had 31 hits in 1964. Since its opening, there have been more than 10 million downloads of their music and they have sold more than 2 million copies.

According to People magazine, Glee was suppose to be about "a group of misfit kids that find their heart, soul and voice (plus friendship and romance) by joining a competitive glee club led by an unfailingly kind Spanish teacher. But when the doors of WMHS opened wide, it soon became clear that Glee-with its mix of irresistible music, sharp comedy, and the instant uplift of a pep rally-had the potential to create pop culture pandemonium."

The show consists of 10 kids that are, in the show, 17 or 18 years old and a few key teachers. The kids which are really actors and actresses ranging from ages 23 to 28 are a cross reference of every kind of stereotyped individual today. The main cast includes:

+ Rachel is the over achieving type A Diva personality
+ Finn is the not-so-smart-football player and the supposed father of Quinn's baby
+ Kurt just came out of the closet with his gay nature and whose father is struggling with that reality
+ Mercedes is the "plus sized," no nonsense minority
+ Quinn is the hot cheerleader that got pregnant and lied about who the father was
+ Puck, the cool "sex symbol" kid, is a blend of the Jewish and Catholic heritages and the real father of Quinn's baby
+ Artie is geeky handicapped kid that performs every week in a wheel chair
+ Tina (who was adopted at the age of 3 from Korea in real life) also plays a minority
+ Brittany and Santana round out the balance of the Glee Club girls
+ Sue Sylvester is the arrogant, track-suit wearing celebrity and single teacher who has it out for the recently divorced Mr. Shuester and the Glee Club in general
+ Mister Will Shuester, the head of the Glee Club and Spanish teacher has the hots for Emma, another teacher and eventually divorces his wife

So then, is Glee really an accurate reflection on today's culture or is it make believe, or perhaps a combination of both? This show, which is wildly successful and has a teen cult following in just one short season, portrays today's "normal" youth and the high school experience as being one where kids are having sex, the cheerleader is getting pregnant, there is gay male lead, its ok to show a few girl-kissing-girl scenes, it's ok for one teacher that started out married (and is now divorced) to flirt with and maybe fall in love with another teacher, and there are so many other by- lines such as the perverted or odd relationship between Sue and Mr. Schuster, that the hits just keep on coming.

So, again I ask, is this show a reflection of today's reality or is it pushing a new standard of "norm" onto everyone watching? Is the popularity of the show only to today's teens who are in love with it or to the parents, or both? The more our culture accepts this and rewards this new "norm" with all sorts of awards and high viewership, the more the line of what's accepted gets pushed from the right move to the center.

As the opening comment in this chapter infers, what one generation "tolerates" the next one "embraces." The culture portrayed on Glee is maybe being tolerated by the baby boomer generation but it is certainly being embraced by Gen-X, Gen-Y and the Millenniums. What we need to keep in mind is that inch-by-inch, what was once considered not so acceptable is now our norm in our culture.

The same holds true in the digital worlds of our kids. Pretty soon our 6-year-old kids will all have phones, everyone will have a Facebook or social network site, sexting will be common place, and life will move on! Or maybe we can step in and manage this metamorphosis a little more closely?

12

THE "NEW" BIRDS AND THE BEES

Any parent living in America today with grown kids or older teens, have all had to deal with that uncomfortable "birds and the bees" talk with their child.

According to Wikipedia, the term "The birds and the bees" is an English-language idiomatic expression which refers to courtship and sexual intercourse, and is usually used in reference to teaching someone, often a young child, about sex and pregnancy. The phrase is evocative of the metaphors and euphemisms often used to avoid speaking openly and technically about the subject.

According to tradition, the birds and the bees is a metaphorical story sometimes told to children in an attempt to explain the mechanics and consequence of sexual intercourse through reference to easily observed natural events. For instance, bees carry and deposit pollen into flowers, a visible and easy-to-explain example of male fertilization. Another example, birds lay eggs, a similarly visible and easy-to-explain example of female ovulation.

Regardless of what the term actually means or at what age it should be delivered, there is no question that the person or persons that delivered the message was either the mom or the dad…the parents. While some may have hoped that the school would jump in there or maybe they would learn it from their friends, the reality for us baby boomers is that this "talk" was our responsibility and no one else's.

Today, in addition to the birds and the bees talk about sex, there now needs to be a birds and bees talk about sexting, cyber bullying and sex predators. In the bigger sense, this is about the dangers of the digital world. Parents need to sit down before they hand over a cell phone or Facebook account on the family computer to their young teen and have the "other" birds and the bees talk. This talk should not be done in a haphazard or random way either.

In fact, when researching for this book, I saw one study that indicated that 22% of young kids between 6-9 own a cell phone. As they got older, 60% between 10-14 and 84% of the rest of the teens are given cell phones. When I first read this study, I said to myself, are you kidding? What possible reason could a 6-year-old need a cell phone? Well the main reason given was for security or safety purposes. But once in their hands, they too become possible targets of sex predators and the rest of the stuff that happens on cell phones.

Parents need to do some advance planning and have a script or outline to follow to make sure all of the points are touched. They need to have statistics and information with them that discuss the issues and the consequences of their kid's actions. For example, a well thought out discussion should review the positive uses of the internet, computers, cell phones and technology in general. Then a transition needs to focus on the bad things happening out there as well. Of course current examples such as sexting and the subsequent prosecutions need to be presented, but at its core, parents need to talk about personal integrity and reputation and what happens if those are lost though bad decisions.

I always told our boys that they needed to anticipate a situation that they may encounter in advance of the event, and then, have a series of positive reactions in mind on how they could respond. Then, when put in those situations for real, they might avoid doing something wrong. Often, our young kids have to make a decision in a split second and without any time to think about good from bad decisions and then before you know it, the deed has already been done and it's too late to take it back.

There are many resources available to help with these new digital talks but if you don't have the talk at all, you are leaving this up to the culture trends. If you open your eyes and watch what is going on, you will certainly want to make sure that you take the bull by the horns and educate your kids yourself.

Don't leave it up to someone else. This is squarely the responsibility of you…the parents!

13

IS THIS BIG BROTHER?

According to Wikipedia, "Big Brother" is a fictional character in George Orwell's novel 1984. He is the enigmatic dictator of Oceania a totalitarian state taken to its utmost logical consequence - where the ruling elite ('the Party') wields total power for its own sake over the inhabitants.

In the society that Orwell describes, everyone is under complete surveillance by the authorities, mainly by telescreens. The people are constantly reminded of this by the phrase "Big Brother is watching you", which is the core "truth" of the propaganda system in this state.

Since the publication of 1984 the term "Big Brother" has entered the lexicon as a synonym for abuse of government power, particularly in respect to civil liberties.

Most people think of Big Brother in a negative context such as the negative feelings like the government is watching over us against our will. When someone feels the loss of freedom or that they are constantly being watched, often they say the "Big Brother" is watching.

As I talked to parents across the country about the dangers of cyber bullying and sex predators in particular, and about the tools that parents have available to them to help protect their kids, a small percentage of parents object to the use of such techniques or tools to monitor their kids.

Why? Why do these parents feel that using a device or tool that could possibly keep their kids from falling prey in the arms of a 42-year-old sex predator is a bad thing? Or why is it that a certain device that protects your 12-year-old daughter when she decides to send or receive a nude text of herself or her boyfriend is a bad thing?

I know there is a small population of people out there that believe that their kids are good and that they have brought them up just fine and resorting to such an action as monitoring certain components of their kid's digital worlds is distasteful. But let me just say this... You can't control all of the people in your children's lives and what they all do. There are 500 million people on Facebook alone for example, and it has become a favorite way for sex offenders to connect with their prey. And yes, I use the word prey. Or maybe victims would also be another good word.

These criminals data mine literally hundreds of thousands of kids' email accounts and often send out a hundred emails a day hoping for that one vulnerable lonely kid to respond. And when they do, watch out…there is no stopping them. They will "friend your child" and do whatever they can until they eventually ask them if they want to meet in real life. Many times this happens within only a few weeks.

As parents, we certainly often give our children the benefit of the doubt and think they are great kids. But a simple slip up and you never know what can happen.

While some may refer to this as Big Brother, in these cases I am happy to have a Big Brother helping or watching, and I know you will too!

14

WHAT DO I DO NOW?

If you go to a parents' internet safety workshop, you will find that a good number of the people that attend a meeting are ones that have children that have already had a problem. Their child may have already had contact with an internet predator, or may have texted an inappropriate photo to a friend that has been passed around the school, or their 12-year-old is being bullied and they don't know what to do.

Why is human nature such that more times than not, we wait until after the damage has been done to do something about it? Why can't we, as parents, decide once and for all that this risky behavior is simply not going to be tolerated and do something about it now... in advance, versus after the fact.

I Googled the words, "RIP TEENS" (rest in peace) and got 3,510,000 results. When you go to YouTube and do the same, you will find that there is a whole a section called "RIP teens: site." In fact there were 10,400 results of families and friends that put together four to five minute emotional music videos packed with remembrance photos of all of the great times had with their teen friends or family members that have lost or taken their lives way too early. Wow, just watch some of these videos…very, very, very emotional!

When you add to this the number of kids cyber bullied every day, the number of teens victimized by predators, and the number of teens texting nude photos or erotic messages to each other, isn't it time to decide that something has to be done to reverse these horrendous trends?

I am not talking about doing one internet safety workshop a year at school or posting something to a website with a bunch or statistics, or watching a three to five minute "60 Minutes" talk show type of presentation.

I am talking about a grass roots effort to address these issues in such a way that our culture starts to change. I may be naïve in thinking that this is possible, but go talk to a parent that has lost a child that committed suicide. Or one that is trying to deal with the emotional scars of their 13-year-old daughter whose nude photo was posted on the web and then sent to most everyone in her middle school.

These types of events are growing in frequency, not the other way around. In order for a grass roots type of effort to happen, all of the following has to happen (and more):

1. **The effort needs to start at home:** parents need to be educated themselves first so they know what they are dealing with. No more putting your heads in the sand.

2. **Tools:** Parents need to take advantage of all of the "tools" available to them. There are programs and devices out there that can be purchased for an affordable price that that deter, detect, or stop risky behavior. Do you think you teen would send a nude photo for example, if they thought mom or dad could see it too?

3. **Education:** Parents need to "be in the know." Learn about Facebook. Get your own account and understand how it works. Know what a "tweet" is and be ready to talk to your child about to use them. Understand the statistics and how to talk about them.

   The Children need to be in the know too. They need to know about the dangers they are about to partake in and the consequences of those actions. They need to know the laws in their state pertaining to sending or receiving underage pornographic photos. This is not just a parent issue, it's a while family issue.

4. **Engage:** You can buy all of the software or devices in the world, but nothing will take the place of a regular and active dialogue

and conversation with your child. Sure the technology will help, particularly when you don't have control of others, like predators going after your kid, but a knowledgeable child is the best defense against unacceptable behavior.

5. **Schools**: the administrators, teachers, and staff, need to develop policies and training programs as to how to address risky behaviors at their school. They need to develop "Zero Tolerance" policies, communicate them to the students and parents, and then enforce them.

   They need to be proactive and not reactive and these changes need to become part of the school culture, not just an occasional assembly that happens for an hour. I am sure if you visited Mentor High School, the entire community has a 360-degree view of how to deal with these issues now that they have lost four of their precious students to suicide. **PTA's and PTO's** could be perhaps one of the greatest avenues to make the biggest impact in today's culture. Here parents can join together on a monthly basis and strategize on how to build a long range plan, how to execute it, and then how to monitor and makes changes as needed to the big picture.

6. **Law Enforcement**: A team of us participated in an evening program for the PTA of Fort Zumwalt, Missouri school system early in the year. Presenting that night included: the school administrators, local law enforcement officers, a judge that presided over the Megan Meier's case, and our team. After hearing what the criminal penalties are in the

state of Missouri for sexting (as an example), every parent and child needs to know these facts.

Hearing it from the officers that may arrest you or the judge that may run the trial was extremely impactful. These basic messages and facts need to get out to each and every family and child in every community in America.

7. **News Community**: If you turned on the TV over the past year you would have undoubtedly seen one of the national stories about the various suicides due to cyber bullying or the girls returned from being kidnapped. You couldn't miss those, they were one weekly. The news community needs to take up this cause and make it part of their regular broadcasts. They need to consider putting links on their websites to educate their listeners and make available news stories in their communities versus just the "big national stories."

8. If you watch the news portion of a local evening broadcast, much of the non-sports and weather segments are about fires, murders, or single stories of interest. These need to be reported but the issues dealing with cyber bullying, sexting, and sex predators we are talking about, are everywhere. They impact everyone, not just an occasional murder victim. A regular commitment to address these issues needs to be part of our news community.

9. **Local Corporate America and businesses:** We have a number of large public corporations and banks that have

taken up the cause of protecting our kids and are looking at providing tools for free to their employees or customers. Many of the large corporations also have foundations with large amounts of funds in there to help with grants and other worthwhile causes. What better use of these funds than protecting the future of our kids? CEO's and business owners…join the grass roots effort.

10. **The Non-Profit Community:** Like Corporate America, non-profits too can get on the bandwagon. There are over a million non-profits in America today. Many of them work in the exact space that are focused on helping kids or could easily add a component to their mission to include addressing these issues. These non-profits often have volunteers and most are on the front lines. That is, they are in the schools, or in the homes of families and are positioned perfectly to make a difference.

So, let's summarize…in today's "Friend Me" generation, the "I" from the title of this chapter, What do "I" Do Now, is not solely addressed to the parents…it's way more. It's a grass roots culture change. This can only be done with the coordinated help of the parents, children, schools, law enforcement, corporate America, non-profits, and the news communities, all working together, hand in hand.

Again, plain and simple…there needs to be a grass roots effort, execution at all levels, and accountability like never before. The stake here are high…and our kids are at risk!

15

TOOLS FOR PARENTING

A s parents, we look to many different tools and resources to help us in this quest to manage the digital worlds and fears of our kids that this new technology is creating.

Here are just some of the tools and resources that you need to check out:

Computer Software and Filters:

There are a number of very good programs and software packages that can be purchased to help protect your children. One such package has a very useful on-line tool that is downloaded to your computer. You are given a dashboard that allows you to load all of the cell phone numbers and all of the Facebook or MySpace accounts of each of your children. Each day everything that goes in and out of their digital worlds is sent through a filtering process and you are emailed "warnings" that identify possible risky behavior.

So for example, if a registered sex predator's phone number shows up trying to connect with your kid, a warning email is triggered. Or if abusive cyber bullying type of language is transmitted back and forth, you will again see a warning email.

In addition, the system comes with a live GPS tracking component, which allows you to see on your own dashboard, exactly where your child is at any given point on time.

You can learn more about these tools at www.whereourkidsmatter. com.

Sex Offenders:

State Sex-offender Registry Websites

Visit the following sites to find lists of registered sex offenders in each state.

- U.S. Department of Justice National Sex Offender Public Registry
- http://www.fbi.gov/hq/cid/cac/registry.htm
- http://www.ice.gov/graphics/predator/sexoffenders.htm

Family Watchdog

Here is a great all around site that helps with quite a few resources particularly in the area of sex offenders.

+ **www.familywatchdog.us**

National Center for Missing and Exploited Kids

This is perhaps the number one rated site on the internet today. It has great resources from information, to blogs, to tools for schools and families.

+ **www.missingkids.com**

Cyber Bullying research Center

Here is one of the best resources for all aspects of cyber bullying. There are presentations, blogs, guides, real life stories, and much more.

+ **www.cyberbullying.us**

Here is a list of the top 50 Text Acronyms that every parent should get to know:

+ **8** - Oral sex
+ **1337** - Elite -or- leet -or- L337
+ **143** - I love you
+ **182** - I hate you
+ **1174** - Nude club

- **420** - Marijuana
- **459** - I love you
- **ADR** - Address
- **AEAP** - As Early As Possible
- **ALAP** - As Late As Possible
- **ASL** - Age/Sex/Location
- **CD9** - Code 9 - it means parents are around
- **C-P** - Sleepy
- **F2F** - Face-to-Face
- **GNOC** - Get Naked On Cam
- **GYPO** - Get Your Pants Off
- **HAK** - Hugs And Kisses
- **ILU** - I Love You
- **IWSN** - I Want Sex Now
- **J/O** - Jerking Off
- **KOTL** - Kiss On The Lips
- **KFY** -or- K4Y - Kiss For You
- **KPC** - Keeping Parents Clueless
- **LMIRL** - Let's Meet In Real Life
- **MOOS** - Member Of The Opposite Sex
- **MOSS** - Member(s) Of The Same Sex
- **MorF** - Male or Female
- **MOS** - Mom Over Shoulder
- **MPFB** - My Personal F*** Buddy
- **NALOPKT** - Not A Lot Of People Know That
- **NIFOC** - Nude In Front Of The Computer
- **NMU** - Not Much, You?
- **P911** - Parent Alert

- **PAL** - Parents Are Listening
- **PAW** - Parents Are Watching
- **PIR** - Parent In Room
- **POS** - Parent Over Shoulder -or- Piece Of Sh**
- **PRON**- porn
- **Q2C** - Quick To Cum
- **RU/18** - Are You Over 18?
- **RUMORF** - Are You Male OR Female?
- **RUH** - Are You Horny?
- **S2R** - Send To Receive
- **SorG** - Straight or Gay
- **TDTM** - Talk Dirty To Me
- **WTF** - What The F***
- **WUF** - Where You From
- **WYCM** - Will You Call Me?
- **WYRN** - What's Your Real Name?
- **ZERG**- To gang up on someone

INTERNET SAFETY WORKSHOPS:

Call your schools or look on their websites for workshops being offered in your area. Many states are putting laws into effect mandating a minimum amount workshop offered by the schools each year. There are also many non-profits, PTA/PTO organizations, Rotary's, Kiwanis organizations, private companies and government entities that offer some form of internet workshop.

If you can't find one, go ahead and contact one of the groups offering them and see if you can help get one into your school or community. You can Google: "cyber bullying" or "sex predators" and find a number of books, DVD's, and other valuable materials and resources that can help.

Live web casts:

The US Department of Health and Human Services can be found at www.hhs.gov.

Through MCHCOM.com which stands for Maternal and Child Health website they do live webcasts and have multi-media presentations on cyber bullying and other related topics.

16

CLOUD PARENTING...
A CALL TO ALL PARENTS!

Parents, we have seen throughout this book that our kids are in the middle of a culture shift "tsunami."

You have all heard the phrase, "there's an 800 pound elephant in the room," but how does that apply to parents protecting their kids?

First, the phrase "There's an elephant in the room" is an English idiom, meaning, "an obvious truth is being ignored or goes unaddressed." Put another way, this expression is really saying that there is an obvious problem or risk that no one wants to discuss. It is based on the idea that if an 800 pound elephant were really in the room, it would be impossible to overlook; thus, the people in the room who pretend the elephant is not there have made a choice to ignore it. They are choosing to concern themselves with tangential or small and irrelevant issues rather than deal with the looming big one.

Well, today our kids are in the middle of a social shift like no other time before in our history and to a large extent, the parents are choosing to ignore the dangers of what is happening. When this tsunami started and how long it will last is anyone's guess, but make no mistake, our kids, and in turn our families are looking this shift squarely in the eye.

At the start of 2011, there were over 500 million Facebook users and some 200 million MySpace users. 98% of adult Americans owned cell phones and we parents are buying smart phones and iPads for our 6-year-olds under the heading of "it protects them while at pre-school or it's really educational."

As we now see, teens sent an average of 3,600 text messages in 2010, up from 3,300 the year before. There were 41 million iPhones in the market and 20 million Android smart phones. 3G speeds were 10 times faster than their predecessors and the first of the 4G phones are now being marketed boasting speeds 10 times faster than the 3G technologies.

In 2010, there were 1.8 trillion SMS text messages sent in America and 55 billion MMS media messages sent. Apple launched its App Store through iTunes in July of 2008 and amazingly in just about 2½ years, they reached their 10 billionth download on January 22, 2011. Wow!

In 2010, the average teen spent six hours on computers and cell phones in the course of a day, and now we even see them sleeping with their devices so as not to miss a call or text at 2 a.m.

At the 2010 Consumers Electronic Show in Las Vegas, new smart phones and tablets were put on display in such numbers that you almost needed a "Picking the Right Cell Phone for Dummies" manual to figure out which tablet or smart phone device was best for you. There are even new cell phones coming out with two screens.

So, again, what does all of this mean to you and me as parents?

Here's the answer: What this means is that technology, with all of its many dangers, are taking over the lives of our kids, and right before our very eyes. And, what are we as parents doing about it… in more cases than not…ignoring this wave and in many cases, embracing it.

We are not doing this on purpose, but sometimes the lack of addressing issues is far worse than addressing them head on and trying to fight what might seem to be an uphill battle to effectuate a permanent change. Not sure what I mean? Well ask yourself these questions:

Do you continue to buy the latest smart phone and give them to your kids at a much younger age? Are you being pressured daily by your kids to allow them to have one or more Facebook accounts, and at a younger age? Are you upgrading your cell phone service to faster internet speeds? Do you allow your kids to have their phones and to text at the dinner table, during conversations, watching TV together, in the car, in the morning, on the way to school, at night and pretty soon in the shower too? (Hopefully not).

Today, our kids are meeting on line, talking on line, fighting on line, breaking up on line and in some weird way having sex on line. They send nude photos of each other, well, at least, one in four that will admit to it in a confidential survey. In school and now on line, our "innocent little Bobby or Susie" will cyberbully other kids to a point where teen suicides are running rampant as the victims try to cope with being the target of this " bully crap" 24 hours a day.

And, as our kids are connected on line all of the time, everywhere, they are now easy pray for sex predators who are data mining the four corners of the internet just waiting for your young innocent child to slip up just once and become vulnerable. When that slip up happens, then they have "got you."

We saw that there are over 1 million registered sex offenders in America today. These are the ones that have committed a crime, have been caught and convicted and have been required by the law to register with local law enforcement. How many more predators are out there that have not been caught? I suspect the real numbers are in the tens of millions.

Our kids, simply stated, don't stand a chance against these evil predators whose sexual desires and perverted passions of appetite need to be filled. They will stop at nothing. They will prowl until they succeed and then guess what, afterwards, they will start all over again with the next victim. Some statistics show that registered sex offenders have had an encounter with an average of 117 kids. Even if this was wrong and it was only five kids, well, that's five kids too many!!!

Imagine this picture for just a moment. If there are 1 million registered sex offenders and if the average offender just had an encounter with five or ten kids, that's five to ten million of our kids being impacted in a horrible way. Way too many!!!

Getting back to the idea of the tsunami, while it is easy to point blame on the sex offenders, consider this. If it is true that one in four teens have sent or received a nude or semi nude photo of himself or herself or from someone else, and if there are some 47 million teens today, that means that in any given year there are some 10-15 million nude photos of teens floating around the Internet. And in this case, it's not the sex offenders driving these actions; it's the kids themselves.

So parents, have I gotten your attention yet? Maybe yes, maybe no?

Okay, so here's the reality we are seeing as we go around the country doing seminars and workshops.

I call it the "Head in the Sand Theory." When we talk to many of the parents, here's what we hear you saying to us in response to this growing problem: "Oh no, not my son or daughter? I have raised young Johnny or young Sally to be such a good kid…. they would never do that stuff." Or, we hear something like, "Yes, that stuff is probably going on and maybe my kids are involved, but I simply don't know what to do about it." In many cases, the people coming to seminars are the parents of kids who have already had a problem...so now they are in a "what do I do now" mode, after it's too late.

So as this tsunami is happening right in front of your eyes you can choose to ignore this tidal wave or you can "get your heads out of the sand and into the cloud"...the "Internet Cloud" that is.

I call this new breed of parenting..."Cloud Parenting." We will address in the next chapter what Cloud Parenting really means.

17

CLOUD PARENTING

First, what exactly is the Cloud? Many of you have heard this phrase and there are now commercials on TV that talk about the Cloud. According to Wikipedia, the Cloud refers to the shared servers and services, software, and access to computers and other devices on demand similar to how we would access an electricity grid.

So long as you are connected to the internet you can access hundreds of thousands, if not millions, of resources. No longer will we need lots of storage on our hand held devices or computers, as they will simply become an access tool to the resources of the Cloud and the internet.

Cloud parenting, is not a term that is found in Webster's Dictionary or even in Wikipedia. It's a concept that I have coined as a metaphor for what I think parents need to be concerned with going forward as it relates to how parents deal with the digital wave that has come and will be here permanently.

I liken Cloud Parenting to a "3-legged stool." There are really three basic components to build a strong foundation, as in a 3-legged stool.

First, awareness…parents need to become aware of what the realities out there really are. Get your head in the game.

Second, execution…parents and our communities need to decide to develop a plan and execute it.

Third, results…parents need see to see and enjoy measurable results.

The three legs then are:

1. Awareness 2. Execution 3. Results.

Lets take a closer look at each one.

Awareness:

It is no longer going to be acceptable to simply make everyone aware of the problems. Last year, it seemed like virtually every week there was a new tragedy being played out on live TV or cable channels. We saw news show after news show chronicle hangings and shootings of cyberbullied kids, kidnappings and the raping of young women by demented men who take them for their child brides and have babies, to 14-year-old boys being convicted of crimes for sending a nude photo of his "then" or perhaps "former" girlfriend to his buddies on the football team.

Let me say this...we would have to be living on a deserted island to not be aware of these horrific events. But what are we actually doing to prevent this? Do we as parents really think and believe that this could be happening to our very own kids? Or do we think it is something that just happens on TV to someone else or some other community?

Question for you: Do you as a parent engage your young kids in a meaningful conversation about these events in a way that effectuates any meaningful change? I suspect the answer is most likely "no." More likely than not, if it was talked about at all, it was a passing conversation along the lines of, "Can you believe this or that happened in this or that town to those families?"

Yes, awareness is important, but it is simply the first step. in the process. It is far from the solution.

Execution:

The first book I wrote is called *"There's a Fine Line."* It introduces how there is often a very fine or thin line between winning or losing, finishing first or second, or just achieving your personal best. As I watched those individuals that had successes, what was perfectly clear was that their success was not by accident. It was by hard work, carefully planned out and executed. What good is a plan that never happens? It's not worth the paper it's written on, is it?

Execution, or the lack thereof, can be best seen in our many New Year's resolutions we make each and every year. We have all been there: lose 15 pounds, stop eating chocolate, no more cigarettes or drinking, exercise 30 minutes a day, pray for 15 minutes each day, spend more time with family, take a vacation, and on and on.

Well, what is the difference between desiring the results and actually achieving them? In a word, it's execution. Executing a plan involves a well thought out strategy that becomes habit and part of your thought process. It's not easy to change who you are or to change your habits.

Execution starts by first outlining the end goal and then developing a plan of action or attack. If you write down exactly how you will achieve the goal, step by step, then I venture to say that you will have a better chance of achieving the desired results. Also, the plan itself is not enough. You will need WILL POWER as well as DESIRE. Permanent change will not happen by accident, it will happen by hard work and committed activity and action.

Results: (measurable)

Now that you are aware of what needs to be done, and now that you have developed a plan of execution, and now that you have begun your quest to make a permanent change, how then do you measure results in this war against digital dangers?

That's a good question, isn't it? This year we formed a new nonprofit called Where Our Kids Matter Foundation. This organization is dedicated to beginning a grass roots effort to promote a permanent and meaningful change in society to help parents with tools, resources, and encouragement to address the digital dangers in this new world.

As with any major effort, some change seems "fast and furious" and other change comes so slow that it almost goes undetected, kind of like turning the Titanic. Whether it's fast or it's deliberate, if we can't see measurable results, then it will be like chasing our tails. As I get older and perhaps wiser, I am beginning to realize that the slow grass roots type of effort is far more effective long term.

As I have been all throughout the country, observing and interacting on these issues, I have identified 8 parts of any local community that form the basis of that society. I call these the "8 Points of Light." Let's take a closer look at these in the next chapter.

18

8 POINTS OF LIGHT

In my opinion, there are eight contact points that every child (and family) will have in their everyday life. These are people, organizations, institutions, and places that will impact and imprint our children on how they develop over time.

I also believe that it is now more important than ever, to bring all of these "Points of light" together in a grass roots effort to make a PERMANENT AND LASTING POSITIVE CHANGE FOR THE GOOD. We want our kids to walk in the light and not the darkness…correct?

Whether it is stopping in its tracks cyberbullying, or preventing sexting of nude photos, or preventing sex predators from achieving their ultimate goals, this surely will take a well-conceived and coordinated effort of the follow eight components of every community.

KIDS

A Kid's first point of contact is often other kids. Everybody, kid or not, feel like they are out of place. So we look to each other for advice and what to do. As peers we need to have positive, caring and respectful attitudes to get rid of cyberbullying, sending inappropriate photos, and promoting safe use of the internet.

PARENTS & FAMILY

As parents, it doesn't often seem like kids view us in a positive light anymore. However, think back to when you were a kid. Did you ever think your parents had the right answer and did you ever want to listen to them? It is a parent's job to stay informed and connected to their kids' worlds, even if it is digital.

SCHOOLS & TEACHERS

As teachers and school administrators, we have the responsibility to keep our kids safe and educated. Parents want to entrust their kids to the school's safekeeping. When teachers and schools see harmful behavior, they should have the ability to intercede in a positive manner.

NON-PROFITS/CHURCHES & SYNAGOGUES

There are hundreds of thousands of organizations like Where Our Kids Matter Foundation and Project Love that are great points of light in a kid's life. Together with local churches and synagogues, these organizations can help develop positive attitudes and change negative behaviors. It is also the responsibility of these organizations to help parents as much as they help kids.

NEWS MEDIA

Kids today are media-holics, whether they believe it or not. Media greets them when they wake up and is in their face throughout the day. Just like reporters are supposed to be unbiased, media has the responsibility to encourage kindness, caring and respect through all mediums of communication. Media needs to be part of the solution, not just a transmitter of information.

LAW ENFORCEMENT

Some kids never run into the law. But the law still plays a very important role in a child's life. The law is what keeps kids safe from potentially dangerous activities. It is law enforcement's responsibility to get the word out to parents and the other points of light that information and knowledge is power. Know the laws and consequences of your actions.

LOCAL CORPORATE AMERICA

Local Corporate America, our everyday businesses, have a huge impact as well on our kids. Apart from the schools and home, kids hang out at local restaurants and movie theaters, and many local stores. They see billboards, television ads, hear radio commercials… all from local businesses. America's businesses have the responsibility to promote change in the lives of kids being bullied and can also help financially.

POLITICIANS

As politicians we have the responsibility to make informed and educated decisions. We need to pass fair legislation that effectively helps kids in need. These new laws need to promote prevention in advance of bad behavior and also need to give schools new tools and ways to effectively deal with day-to-day negative actions. We need to constantly engage issues our children face, as they are our future.

If these eight points of light all came together in a well coordinated grass roots effort, it is my belief beyond a doubt, that our kids, families, and communities, can reverse and even stop entirely this negative tsunami of bad behavior.

It won't be easy and it may come with a price, but I think we will all agree that our kids are well worth the fight!

19

A FINAL WORD TO PARENTS

Some of you may have heard of the famous defense attorney from Wyoming, Gerry Spence. Attorney Spence is known for his flamboyant closing arguments and his southwestern style of dress as he is often seen in court wearing a cowboy hat and a tan buckskin leather jacket. According to Wikipedia, Gerry Spence is a registered trial lawyer in the United States and claims to have never lost a criminal case with a trial by jury in over 50 years that he practiced law.

One of Gerry's famous closing arguments to the jury goes something like this. He would walk slowly over to the jury box and get as close as he could get to stare the jurors squarely in the eye and then he would hold out his hands and cup them together as if to be hiding something inside them. And then he would say the following: "I want you to think that inside my cupped hands is a small delicate bird and it represents my client. Today, you and you alone will have the power to either crush this bird (as he mashes his hands together) or you can find him innocent and let him go free (as he opens his hands in a motion to let the bird fly free).

The point he is making is that the power of the outcome of his client rest solely in the hands of the jury and no one else...not the other lawyers, the judge, the reporters...not anyone else. It's in the hands of the jurors.

Like this metaphor being used here, so too we as parents have the sole responsibility to mange the dangers of the internet and our kids digital worlds. It's not a job that we relegate to the hands of the schools, or the churches, or our kid's friends...it's solely in our hands...the PARENTS.

We can elect to ignore those tough discussions with our 10 or 12-year-olds about trying to get to 500 friends on Facebook (many of which they don't even know) or having a frank and stern conversation about the dangers and ramifications of sending or receiving a nude text of themselves to a friend they are trying to impress.

Or we can sit down and create a new standard of communication with them in this digital world and create in essence a new "social contract" of sorts. This should be the type of new dialogue you have..."If you want a cell phone or a Facebook account, here are the new rules..."

If you wait until your child has met up with a predator on line, or has sent s nude photo and it's being passed all over school, it's too late and the damage has already been done. Many of the folks that attend an internet safety workshop are not those with kids that have had a problem or issue yet, but rather those parent that are dealing with the aftermath of something that has already happened. And believe me, that a very painful and difficult time for them, their family, their schools, and communities.

So what exactly can be done then? I have found that our young kids will fall into one of the following categories:

1. **Very young teens with no Facebook account or cell phone.** These kids are the ones hounding you every day to open an account or to buy a cell phone. "But mom, all of the kids at school have one…I am so embarrassed to be the only one." These young pre-teens will be relentless until they finally wear you down and you give in and get them a phone or Facebook account.

For sure, you need to sit them down and have a very detailed conversation. You need to establish the rules of their phones and of their Facebook accounts.

2. **Young Teens or pre-teens that have recently received a cell phone or Facebook account.** These are the teens that have a relatively new mobile device that maybe they got for their 13th birthday, or maybe because they got good grades. But now, they are part of the new teens community that are

on their way to sending 3600 text messages a month (the average for teens today).

Since these youngsters already have a phone, you may have to establish some new rules which may be hard since they have had the phone for a year, maybe two, and now you are coming in and changing "the deal" in their minds, even though you may not have had a deal in the first place.

You need to discuss the dangers out there and now explain that they need to know in advance how to handle each situation. For example, if someone sends them a nude text, how do you handle that? If someone they don't know asks to friend them, how do you respond?

These and many other topics are invaluable conversations to engage your young teen in and sooner than later.

3. **Older teens that have had cell phones for some time now.** These are the kids that are fully engaged…they text 3600 messages a month, have 500 to 2000 Facebook "friends" (more than the number of kids in their high school) and in many cases take their phones to bed with them so as not to miss a call or text. Well, this is clearly the most difficult age group to deal with.

These kids are fully and emotionally involved into their digital worlds. They are texting their friends on time every nine waking minutes, have a well established network of digital friends and spend on average 38 minutes a day just managing their Facebook accounts. They are very private in their conversations and the last thing they want is to have their moms or dads "checking in on them" or "managing their digital lives."

At the same time, these are the ones that are getting into most of the trouble. They are the ones being cyber bullied 24/7 and then solving their problems by taking their own lives. They are the ones that are sending nude photos and then being prosecuted for child pornography. They are the ones that the on-line sex predators are going after, since they are "easy prey" and often unmonitored by an adult.

So as a parent, how do you handle this situation? When I was 16 the most precious thing to me was my drivers license and the ability to drive my car anywhere. Today, 16-year-olds would give up their cars and freedoms in a heartbeat over losing their cell phones.

Now, having said all of this about the role of the parent, a few chapters earlier we discussed the need for a grass roots effort in America. So assume for a minute that the parents took an entirely more aggressive and active role in addressing the digital dangers and then we added on top of this a consistent and well thought out community wide grass roots effort. Tell me, do you think all of this hard work would make a difference?

I THINK SO!

As a closing statement to this book, lets all go out and go M.A.D.

(make a difference). If we don't make our minds up and motivate ourselves to change, who will?

Let's do it for the sake of our kids and for our communities!

ACKNOWLEDGEMENTS, DISCLOSURES, SOURCES, AND COMMENTARY

The following are the property and trademarks of their respective companies:

1. Facebook
2. Apple
3. Twitter
4. MySpace
5. Chatroulette
6. Wikipedia
7. You Tube

Wikipedia: Numerous uses of information for the book was taken from Wikipedia, which is a free, web-based, collaborative, and multilingual encyclopedia and is supported by the non-profit Wikimedia Foundation. It has17 million articles and has been written collaboratively by volunteers around the world and almost all of its articles can be edited by anyone with access to the site.

Wikipedia was launched in 2001 by Jimmy Wales and Larry Sangerand and has become the largest and most popular general reference work on the internet having 365 million readers.

Facebook: is a social network service and website launched in February 2004 that is operated and privately owned by Facebook, Inc. As of January 2011, Facebook has more than 600 million active users.

Statistics: Multiple statistics are found and posted on the Internet. Many of these statistics were used for illustrative purposes through the book.

Text Lingo: The list of text messages is seen in multiple places on the Internet.

Articles: information from People Magazine October 2010 issue and the People Magazine October 2010 issue and GQ November issue. These magazines are trademarks of their owners.

FBI: Statistics taken from public information found quoted from the Internet.

WPXI: is the registered name of the Pittsburg Television Station.

NBC Dateline News posted results on their program of estimates taken in 2006 of various Sex Predator topics.

National Institute of Mental Health posted the typical number of children exposed to an average registered sex offender and other relevant statistics.

Surveys: the following surveys have been referenced: iSafe survey of 4th-8th graders posted on the internet, Sex and Tech Survey of Teens and Young Adults posted on the internet.

Blogs: are referenced in the book and are Social Media sites written by "bloggers" whom discuss various topics and invite participation.

Big Brother is referenced and is a book written by George Orwell.

RIP is a term meaning "rest in peace" and was used in referencing the many video posted on the site You Tube.

Tools: many tools are referenced in Chapter 15. These tools are referenced as a resource for parents to use. Some of these tools are found on the following sites: www.missingkids.com (National Center for Missing and Exploited Kids), www.familywatchdog. com, various public governmental sites such as the sex offenders registry, www.cyberbullying.us (Cyber Bullying research center), www.hhs.gov (US Department of Health and Human Services).

Gerry Spence is an attorney of law and not associated with the book.